Life and Beth

A play

Alan Ayckbourn

Samuel French — London
www.samuelfrench-london.co.uk

LIFE AND BETH

First presented at the Stephen Joseph Theatre, Scarborough on 22nd July 2008 with the following cast:

Beth Timms	Liza Goddard
Gordon Timms	Adrian McLoughlin
Martin Timms	Richard Stacey
Ella Packer	Ruth Gibson
Connie Bunting	Susie Blake
David Grinseed	Ian Hogg

Directed by Alan Ayckbourn
Designed by Pip Leckenby
Lighting by Kath Geraghty
Music by John Pattison

CHARACTERS

Beth Timms, recently widowed, 50s
Gordon Timms, Beth's late husband, formerly a
          maintenance engineer, 60s
Martin Timms, their son, a car salesman, 30s
Ella Packer, Martin's girlfriend, late 20s
Connie Bunting, Gordon's sister, also a widow, 50s
David Grinseed, a clergyman and a widower, 50s
Man, Police Officer, voice only
Woman, Police Officer, voice only

SYNOPSIS OF SCENES

The action takes place in the living room of Beth and
Gordon Timms' suburban, semi-detached house

ACT I
Christmas Eve. Evening

ACT II
SCENE 1 An hour or so later
SCENE 2 Christmas Day. Around midday

Time — the present

Other plays by Alan Ayckbourn published by Samuel French Ltd

ACT I

A modest sitting/dining room in a fairly modern, semi-detached suburban house. Christmas Eve, evening

There is a dining table, easy chairs, a coffee table, a TV, etc. In one corner there is an empty cat basket bed. A single door leads to the hall and the rest of the house. In one wall there is a service hatch with twin doors connecting to the kitchen. There is also a fireplace with a coal-effect electric fire, next to which there is a set of superfluous fire tongs

Beth, a pleasant woman in her fifties, is sitting on the sofa. Across from her in the armchair sits Connie, about the same age, fidgeting awkwardly

On the coffee table between them are the remains of tea things for two, biscuits, etc. The TV, on low, is playing a carol service from somewhere or other. There is little evidence that it is Christmas time. One or two cards dotted about, nothing more

The women appear to have run out of conversation. Whilst Beth is quite happy with this, it's evidently not a situation that suits Connie

Connie (*after a long pause*) Well …
Beth (*vaguely, agreeing with her*) Mmmmm.
Connie As I say …

A pause

He was remarkable, wasn't he …?
Beth (*vaguely*) Oh, yes …
Connie Treasure. Absolute treasure. They broke the mould … when they … didn't they? Everyone adored him, didn't they? I mean you, you simply worshipped him, didn't you? The ground he stood on?
Beth Yes, I was very fond of him.
Connie Oh, come on, you adored him. We could all see that. No, I mean, face it, Beth, you couldn't have done better, could you? Better than Gordon? As husbands go, I mean … as husbands go …
Beth Yes. Well, he's gone now, hasn't he?

Connie God rest his soul.

Beth Yes.

Connie (*after a pause*) He was a wonderful brother to me, too. My big brother, I called him. I mean, I know I was a little bit older than him but only by a year or so. But I always thought of him as my big brother. I couldn't have asked for better. Always looked out for me, always took care of me. I only had to lift the phone ...

Beth ... yes.

Connie ... he was always at the other end, Gordon. Sorting me out.

Beth Yes, you were often on the phone to him ...

Connie Well, he was my brother. I was his sister. All on my own, wasn't I?

Beth I know.

Connie ... all on my little own ... No. Gordon was always the special one. I know my parents felt he was. I mean, from the minute he was born, almost. I don't think it was just because he was the boy. It would have been the same even if he'd been a ... He was always remarkable ... reading early ... writing ... multiplying in his head, you know ... Me? I couldn't keep up with him. Didn't even try. You know, when I was about eight or nine, it must have been, Dad took me to one side and he said, "Don't get me wrong, Connie. Me and your mum, we still love you, we both still think the world of you but even though you're the eldest, we're going to need you to step aside, love, make room for young Gordon. You're going to have to let him past. Like in a race. He's lapping you, you see, Connie. He's been round three times to your one and he's still passing you ..."

Beth He shouldn't have said that to you.

Connie No, it was true, Dad was being honest, he was only being honest with me ... all the time I was growing up. I could always feel Gordon, breathing down my neck. No, he was like that, my Dad. He always came straight to the point, I admire that in a man ...

Beth Still, it was only his opinion, wasn't it? You never know, you might have come on later ——

Connie Later?

Beth You might have been a late developer, if they'd given you a year or two.

Connie I never developed at all, did I?

Beth Not surprised, after that.

Connie Well, we'll never know now, will we? Nearly forty years ago. I could have been a scientist, couldn't I? Or a surgeon?

Beth (*slightly dubious*) Possibly.

Connie Now look at me. Stocktaking at Porters.

Beth You've done well.

Connie But I could have done better. I know I could. If I hadn't stepped aside for Gordon. He had the best of everything. He had the biggest bedroom. Best education. We all made sacrifices for Gordon.

Beth Well, maybe you shouldn't have done, Connie.

Connie Well, I had no say in it, did I?

Beth I mean, Gordon never became a scientist or a surgeon either, did he?

Connie No. But we all thought he might have been ...

Beth Health and Safety Officer at Twistleton's. That's a far cry from brain surgeon ...

Connie They spent every penny they had on him. I never got my dolls' house. Dad couldn't afford it. Nor a pony. I always wanted a pony. All I got was his hand-me-down tricycle. The day he got his new fairy cycle.

A pause. Connie reflects back gloomily on her life

Beth (*trying to lighten the mood*) Oh well, under the bridge now, isn't it?

Connie That's where I feel my life's gone, Beth. Under the bridge and into the drain ...

Beth (*reflecting; smiling*) Fairy cycle! Think I had a fairy cycle ...

Connie ... into the sewer ...

Beth (*indicating the TV*) Oh, this is a lovely carol, isn't it? It's one of my favourites ... Do you mind if I turn it up a bit?

Beth operates the remote. The volume on the TV increases. Beth hums along with the carol. Connie starts to cry. Beth is aware of this and attempts initially to ignore it. Connie gets louder, eventually competing with the TV. Beth turns off the TV

(*Slightly irritably*) Connie, do try and cheer up, love. Come on now, it's Christmas.

Connie (*tearfully*) It's all right for you, Beth.

Beth What do you mean, it's all right for me? I've just lost my husband, for heaven's sake ...

Connie Yes, and I've just lost a brother ...

Beth You weren't even that fond of him, were you?

Connie I was, I adored him.

Beth You just said he ruined your life ...

Connie What a terrible thing to say. That's a terrible thing to say, Beth, about my brother. About your late husband ...

Beth makes to respond, then checks herself and takes a deep breath

Beth Maybe you'd like to unpack your things? I've put you up in the spare room. I hope that's all right?
Connie Oh, that'll do me. I won't sleep much anyway.
Beth ... I gave it a good airing ...
Connie ... never sleep these days ...
Beth ... I put Martin and his friend Ella in our room ... in my room ...
Connie Your room? Where are you sleeping, then?
Beth I'll have the couch here ...
Connie The couch?
Beth This sofa bed, it pulls out ...
Connie That's not very fair on you, is it ...?
Beth It makes quite a nice little bed, this sofa. We used it a lot in the old days. Whenever we had a full house ...
Connie ... turning you out of your bed ...
Beth ... it's no problem. I'll be up first, it's not a problem ...
Connie ... this is meant to be a break for you ...
Beth ... I'm not sleeping that much lately, either ...
Connie ... we agreed, Martin and I, you're not to lift a finger. It's a Christmas for you to put your feet up. What sort of rest would it be, if you're going to be down here sleeping rough?
Beth It's really rather comfy. Gordon even used to ... at the end, you know, when he couldn't ... cope with the stairs ... before he was ... (*She tails away*)
Connie (*sympathetically*) Yes ...

A silence

Still, it could get a bit chilly down here in the night, couldn't it? Once the heating goes off.
Beth I can always put the fire on.
Connie Be careful you don't gas yourself with the fumes. I was reading, you know, about this entire family ——
Beth It's electric.
Connie Oh. (*She pauses*) Still got his basket, I see.
Beth What?
Connie (*indicating the cat basket*) Wagstaff's basket. Still got it, have you?
Beth Yes.
Connie Just in case he ...?
Beth Comes back.
Connie No sign of him?

Beth No. Day of the funeral he just went out through the cat flap in the kitchen there, never came back. Never came back for his tea.

Connie Oh, well. They say they can sense it, can't they? Animals? They say they hate change almost as much as we do. He probably missed Gordon. He sensed Gordon had gone forever and it upset him so much he ran off ...

Beth He didn't even like Gordon.

Connie Beg your pardon?

Beth Wagstaff couldn't stand him.

Connie Oh, he must have liked Gordon, surely?

Beth He used to hiss at him whenever he came near.

Connie Everybody adored Gordon.

Beth Wagstaff didn't.

Silence

You going to church later on? For the midnight service tonight?

Connie Yes ... I'll go along ... support David, you know ...

Beth Support who?

Connie David Grinseed. The Reverend Grinseed.

Beth Oh, yes ...

Connie I always call him David. He prefers it if his close friends call him David. I know him as David, anyway.

Beth Yes, of course, he did the funeral, didn't he? I'd forgotten his name was David.

Connie Well, it's not everyone he — you have to get to know him for a little while first.

Beth He was very pleasant.

Connie Oh, yes.

Beth It was a nice funeral.

Connie Oh, he always does a good funeral, David. Quiet manner. Sympathetic.

Beth Yes. Have you been to many of them, then?

Connie Beg your pardon?

Beth Funerals? You sound as if you've been to several.

Connie Well ... as I say, I try to support him, you know.

Beth I see.

Connie It's not only funerals. I mean, I go to his weddings as well.

Beth Christenings?

Connie One or two. If I'm not working. I don't join in, you know. I'm just there for support. David's not married. He lost his wife a few years ago. (*Mouthing*) Cancer.

Beth Oh, sad.

Connie So he's just a bit lonely. Currently. Yes, David's a lovely man once you get to know him.

A pause. Connie is a little flustered. Beth stares at her. Connie turns her attention to the tea things

I'd better clear all this, hadn't I?

Beth No, no, Connie, I can easily …

Connie Beth, I've told you, you're doing nothing. You're not lifting a finger 'til New Year's Eve …

Beth I can easily rinse them through ——

Connie (*fiercely*) Sit down! You're to sit down, now!

Beth (*feebly*) You don't even know where anything goes ——

Connie Then you can show me …

Beth What's the point of that? It's just as easy for ——

Connie Sit!

Beth (*sitting; muttering*) It's my house …

Connie Not for the next few days, it's not. You're to treat this place just like a luxury hotel, do you hear?

Connie starts for the door with the tray

Beth Probably should have done that, really …

Connie Done what?

Beth … if we'd thought of it. Gone to a hotel.

Connie (*dubiously*) Oh, I don't think so. I wouldn't fancy that. Not at Christmas-time. Not in a strange hotel.

Beth Might have been rather nice. A bit of an adventure, really …

Connie We don't want adventures at our time of life, do we? Certainly not at Christmas.

The doorbell rings

Beth (*rising*) Oh, that'll be them!

Connie (*putting down the tray*) Don't worry, I'll let them in.

Beth They're early. Traffic must have been good.

Connie Wait there, wait there. Luxury hotel, remember?

Beth (*unconvinced*) Yes …

Connie (*as she goes*) Here goes the chambermaid …

Connie exits

Beth sits for a moment, then rises and stares round the room. Her gaze finally alights on the empty cat bed

Beth Where have you got to then, you little bugger? (*She sighs*) Oh, well.

She turns towards the tea tray where Connie left it. Beth seems intent on taking it out to the kitchen but before she can move to it, the tray jumps slightly, as if shaken, causing the crockery to rattle

(*Startled*) Oh! (*Staring at the tray, puzzled*) That's odd. (*She makes to examine the tea tray but before she can*)

Connie enters, flushed with excitement. She leads in David, a clergyman in his late fifties, at present in official mode, i.e. visiting a recently bereaved parishioner whom he doesn't know terribly well

Connie (*in a hushed tone*) Beth. It's David. Come to see you.
Beth Oh.
David Hallo, Mrs Timms. I'm sorry to burst in on you on Christmas Eve. I just wanted to see how you're doing. I hope this isn't entirely the wrong moment ...
Beth (*a bit flustered*) No. Do come in. We were just ... having tea. Would you care for some?
David No, no, thank you.
Connie You sure, David? It's no trouble ...
David No, please, I know traditionally vicars are always up for free teas ... but not just at present, thank you. If truth be told, the day I've just been having, I could probably do with something stronger ...
Beth Well, there's some beer, I think. I got in some beer for my son.
Connie (*with her*) There's some beer, David ...
David No, that's awfully kind but no thank you. I'm here for a briefest second. I just wanted a quick word with Mrs Timms. I promised her I'd look in weeks ago ... make sure she was coping OK.
Beth Do sit down, won't you?
David Thank you.

David continues to stand. There is a slight pause. David looks at Beth, smiling. Beth smiles at David, rather shyly. Beth looks at Connie. David looks at Connie

Connie (*a little put out*) Well, I'll ... I'd better wash these up, then. (*Picking up the tray*) You just shout if you need anything, David.
David Thank you, Connie.
Connie That's me. Connie cook and chief bottle-washer ...

David laughs politely

I'll just be in the kitchen.

Connie goes out with the tea tray

Beth Please, do sit down Mr — er — Reverend ——

David (*doing so*) David, please. David.

Beth David.

David Everyone calls me David. It's Beth, isn't it? You don't mind if I call you Beth?

Beth Everyone else does ...

David Listen, Beth — I know we met, of course, at the service ——

Beth Oh, yes. Briefly.

David Funerals are always such awkward, emotional occasions. Sometimes I find it's better to leave things a week or two. Just to let the — (*gesturing vaguely*) — the — things to settle a bit.

Beth Yes.

David But I enjoyed our talk together afterwards.

Beth (*frowning*) Did you?

David You don't remember?

Beth I remember a few words, I —— (*She shakes her head*)

David Well, it was more than a few words, we did have quite a chat. You obviously don't remember?

Beth I'm sorry. It was — one of those days, you know. Sorry.

David No, no, why should you? So, Beth. Tell me, how's it been without — er — without — Graham?

Beth Gordon.

David Gordon, I'm sorry. How's life without Gordon? Bit tough still, is it? I imagine it must still be tough. People I spoke to said you were both very close.

Beth Well, it's strange, really. I mean, I miss him, of course. I couldn't not miss him. Gordon. He was always there, you see. 'Til he went.

David Yes, yes. It was a very special marriage, I imagine. And he went quite suddenly, your sister tells me.

Beth Sister-in-law ...

David Sorry.

Beth Connie's Gordon's sister. She's not my sister ...

David Sorry. Bit guilty of not quite doing my homework, I'm afraid. So it all happened suddenly? That must have been the most terrible shock.

Beth Yes, it was quite sudden, really. He had the fall at work, of course ...

David Oh, dear. Now remind me, where did he work?

Beth Twistleton's Engineering. He fell off a ladder. He should never have been up there in the first place, especially not with him being in charge of Health and Safety, but he insisted … Never listened to anyone.

David What was he doing up this ladder?

Beth Trying to rescue this lad. Who should never have been up there either. Not with the lad having vertigo. Gordon clearly told him to come down the ladder at once as he was contravening mandatory Health and Safety procedures. Only he panicked.

David Gordon panicked?

Beth No, the lad panicked. Gordon didn't panic, Gordon never panicked. He climbed up the ladder to rescue the lad. Only this lad was so terrified, his hands were gripped tight to the ladder. And when Gordon tried to lever them open, he fell off.

David The lad fell off?

Beth No, Gordon fell off trying to lever the lad off the ladder. The lad's fingers stayed gripped tight.

David Heavens!

Beth They had to cut the whole ladder down with the lad still clinging to it. Took him and the ladder off to A & E. Eventually they had to operate.

David On the ladder?

Beth No, on the lad. The ladder was cast iron. They had to put the lad under and ease open his fingers from the ladder. He'd gone into spasm, you see.

David Poor lad, poor lad.

Beth Yes, he recovered quickly enough, though.

David Oh, good.

Beth More than Gordon did. He broke his back.

David Oh, that's terrible. How terrible!

Beth That was the start of it. When they finally let him home, practically the first thing he did was to fall off a chair.

David Oh, heavens! Just quietly sitting, was he?

Beth No, he was standing on it. In the kitchen, out there. Trying to fix something, as usual.

David Not the sort of thing he should have been doing with a recently broken back, surely?

Beth He was always fixing things, Gordon. Very keen on DIY.

David Well, you know what they say. Ninety per cent of accidents occur in the home, don't they?

Beth Something like that. Most of them were Gordon's.

David (*looking to change the subject*) Well, anyway …

Beth Have-a-go hero, that's what they called him in the paper.

David Yes, yes …

Beth That's not what I called him. Bloody stupid idiot, I called him. (*After a slight pause*) Sorry.

David Well, you know Beth, most of us do tend to feel angry occasionally with those we love most, don't we? Sometimes it's almost irrational. Possibly because we care so much about them that we grow angry if they injure themselves, we tend to feel their hurt almost as if it were our own. When they finally leave us alone in the world ... particularly a relationship as close as yours ... it's practically a sense of betrayal, isn't it? I know, in my own case, my late wife ... she ... (*He hesitates*) ... I mean it was months, years before I finally ... but I prayed for guidance ... and eventually, Beth, the realization came to me, I saw that, no, this isn't the way I should be remembering her, not with anger or with bitterness, not with resentment ... that wasn't the way. I must let all that go, mustn't I? Rather I should remember her with love. And, finally, after all those endless months of anguish, I found peace and contentment. It's not a matter of forgetting, Beth. Heaven forbid that we should ever forget. It's rather a case of *how* we remember, do you see?

Beth Yes.

David I sense, Beth, that you loved your husband, you loved Gordon more than you loved your own life.

Beth Yes, well, I ...

David And that love was a beautiful and special thing, Beth. The love between a husband and wife can be the most precious there is. Our Lord intended it that way and — aside from our love for Him, of course — the love that exists between a husband and wife is the strongest. But when the day finally comes to say *au revoir* — well, it's rather like that lad with the ladder, isn't it? We need to learn to let go. Release the fingers, relinquish that grip, you see?

Beth Right ... right.

David Because rage, anger, disappointment, frustrated unrequited love, sense of betrayal, they're all negatives, aren't they? There's an old song you know. I don't expect you know it, Beth, probably before your time. I can't remember who wrote the words — possibly Johnny Mercer? Sammy Kahn? It goes something like this: "You've got to ac-cent-tchu-ate the positive ... eliminate the negative ... cling right on to the affirmative ... and don't mess with Mr In-Between." You see?

Beth No, I can't say I know that one.

David is standing quite close to Beth now, their eyes on each other. Silence. A scratching sound can be heard from the kitchen hatch. They become aware of this. David looks puzzled

(*Frowning*) Excuse me, please.

Beth moves swiftly to the hatch and pulls it open to reveal a startled Connie, clutching a milk jug

Connie (*startled*) Oh, sorry!
Beth Sorry, Connie, did you want something?
Connie No, I was just ... wondering ... wondering where this ...
Beth (*brusquely*) In the cupboard over the sink.

Beth closes the hatch abruptly and moves back to David

I beg your pardon, David, you were saying?
David (*vaguely; a little bemused*) Was I? Yes, I ...
Beth Don't mess with Mr ...
David In-Between. Yes.
Beth Yes.
David I hope that's been of help, Beth.
Beth Yes, it's been most helpful, thank you.
David Life is for living. I really believe that.
Beth Oh, yes. I mean that's the reason we're all here, isn't it?
David You're still young — for a woman. You're attractive.
Beth Thank you.
David Life is ahead of you. Seize it with both hands. Make new friends, explore new places. Turn a new page, Gerald is a past chapter ——
Beth Gordon.
David Go on! Push the boat out! Take that dog of yours for a long walk, why don't you?
Beth Dog?
David He's out of his basket, anyway. He's eager to find a way forward. Come on, I bet he hasn't had a walk for days, has he? He's probably even now scratching at the back door, dying for a walk.
Beth He's a cat.
David Well, then ... do whatever you do with cats. Pick it up and cuddle it. Get used to sharing your love again, Beth ...
Beth Wagstaff's gone.
David Who?
Beth The cat. He walked out, he just wandered off.
David Oh dear. How long's it been gone?
Beth About six weeks ago. He left the day of the funeral.
David Ah, well. They say animals often sense things, don't they? They have an instinctive sense of when things aren't all they should be.
Beth I wish he'd told me ...
David Ah. Would that they could speak sometimes.
Beth ... I'd probably have left with him.

David Yes?

Beth But then ... I couldn't do that, could I? Not the day of the funeral ...

David No, we're not like cats, are we?

Beth I can now, though, can't I?

David How do you mean?

Beth Walk away. My life's my own again, isn't it? Free as a bird.

David That's the spirit. (*Smiling at Beth*) Good on yer, Beth.

Beth (*smiling at David*) Thank you.

They stand for a moment looking at each other

David (*awkwardly; shyly*) Beth, would you ... would you mind if I — if I —— ?

Beth Would I mind what, David?

David Would you think it — terribly ... if I —— ?

Beth If you what?

David If I said a prayer for you? Would you mind?

Beth Oh. No, not at all. Why not? I have a Buddhist friend who's chanting for me somewhere. The more the merrier.

David Thank you. These days, some people, they rather object — in principle, you know. Best to check first. (*He clasps his hands and closes his eyes*)

Beth What, now? You're going to say it *now*?

David Yes.

Beth With me here?

David Do you mind?

Beth Might make me feel a bit weird, you know. Hearing myself discussed.

David I promise I'll only say — of course, if you'd rather I ——

Beth No, you carry on, David. Don't mind me.

David prepares to resume his prayer. Beth waits, rather self-consciously. The front doorbell rings

Oh, that's probably them. My son, Martin, and his friend. Would you excuse me a moment ... (*She goes to the door*)

David Of course.

Beth, on her way out, nearly collides with Connie

Beth Oh, beg your pardon, Connie.

Connie (*as she goes*) I'll go, Beth. I'll let them in, don't worry.

Connie exits

Beth Sorry to interrupt you, David. Do carry on.
David Well ... maybe this is ... not the time. I'll save it 'til I get to church.
Beth Perhaps that'd be best. Probably be stronger from there. (*She smiles*)
David (*smiling*) Possibly.

Voices are heard from the hall. A moment passes

Connie comes back in

Connie (*as she enters*) They're here ... they've arrived ...

Martin, in his thirties, enters. Although he is rarely less than ebullient, he is especially so at present, in anticipation of this occasional, somewhat exceptional, meeting with his mother. Unsure of how he'll find Beth's state, he has characteristically opted for seasonal bluster

Martin Knock-knock! We're here! At last! Hallo, Mum! (*He embraces Beth*)
Beth (*reciprocating*) Martin!

David, rather affected by this family reunion, steps back and smiles

Connie remains in the doorway where she is soon joined by Ella, a rather pale, currently red-eyed woman in her late twenties who also stops to witness the meeting of mother and son. Ella has the aura of a woman currently nursing a grievous insult

Martin (*holding Beth at arm's length*) You're looking well, Mum. You're looking fantastic. Isn't she, Auntie Connie? Fantastic.
Connie Oh, yes, considering ...
Martin You both are, you both are.
Connie ... considering, yes.
Martin Sorry we're a bit late. Deviated from the sat nav. Took a detour, got a bit lost.
Beth You're not late.
Martin Someone, who shall remain nameless but certainly wasn't me, misread the map.
Beth I think you've put on weight, son.

Martin Possibly, possibly. (*Indicating Ella*) If I have, then you can
totally blame that one. Mum, this is my friend Ella. Ella, say hallo to
everyone.

Ella smiles; a rather subdued response

Beth Hallo, Ella ...
David (*shyly*) Hallo, there.

Ella gives another of her half-hearted smiles

Martin No word of a lie, this is no exaggeration, Ella is one of the great
cooks in the country ——
Beth Well ...
Martin ... present company always excepted, Mum. Ella is known
locally in Dorchester as the Cholesterol Queen ... I'm joking, I'm
joking, love ...
Beth I hope you are.
Connie Honestly, Martin! You never know with him, do you?
Martin So, I'm warning you in advance, be prepared for a simply
fabulously gastronomic Christmas. No calories spared. Now! Listen!
We're here, we've arrived — no thanks to our map reader here. We're
now going to unload the four by four — we're jammed to the gunnels
— Mum, you're to relax, put your feet up, take it easy. From this
moment on, we're taking over ... You're not to do a single thing from
now on, do you hear? Have you told her that, Auntie Connie? Mum's
to do nothing?
Connie I keep telling her ...
Martin Do nothing. That's an order.
Connie ... not that she listens to me ...
Martin (*turning to leave*) Right. You fit, Ella? Let's get going. Let's
make this place a bit more festive, shall we? (*He notices David for the
first time*) Oh, hallo, squire, where did you spring from?
David Hallo, there.
Beth Oh, Martin this is the reverend — the vicar ——
Connie Martin, this is David.
Martin Oh, how do you do.
David Hallo. David Grinseed.
Martin You stopping for Christmas as well, are you?
David No, no, no ... I was just ——
Beth He's visiting.
Connie David's just visiting.
David Passing through. Checking on — Beth here. Yes, I can see
everything's under control — if you'll excuse me, I'll be ...

Martin Not stopping for a beer?

David No, thank you ...

Martin Something stronger, then? Whisky?

David No. Really, I ——

Martin Little one? Single malt. We brought the single malt, didn't we, Ella? Didn't manage to drop that, did you? Whole carrier bag, full of stuff — Baileys, Apricot Brandy, Tia Maria — right down the stone steps in the car park. Place smelt like a brewery ...

Beth Oh, dear ...

Connie I've done that in my time.

Martin I told her you'll be popular with Mum now. She'll overlook the Baileys and the Apricot Brandy, but she'll never forgive you for the Tia Maria. That's Mum's special tipple, Tia Maria ...

Beth Never mind, doesn't matter. Actually, I think I still have some left over from last year ... Never got round to ... what with ... Anyway, it was never my ... it was more ... he liked a drop, occasionally. I sometimes — joined him, you know ... keep him company ... special occasions ... like this.

Silence

Martin Yes, yes.

Connie Yes.

David (*after a slight pause*) Look, I wonder, if you'd mind — before I go — might I suggest that we all of us share in a brief prayer for Beth — just a short one — together — to remember — (*concentrating for the name*) — her husband ...

Beth (*softly*) Gordon ...

David Yes. And of course your father, Marvin ...

Martin Martin.

David I think that might be a nice idea. Fitting. Especially at this time of year. When we're — when we're all gathered.

Connie Lovely.

Martin Yes. Why not?

Connie makes to kneel down

David (*anticipating Connie*) No, no, we don't need to kneel down. I don't think that's ... If we could simply stand in a circle — a family circle, as it were ...

They all shuffle, rather self-consciously, into a small, tight circle in the middle of the room

That's it ... Dear Lord ——

Martin Should we be joining hands?

David No. This isn't a seance ... just a quick prayer ...

Martin Right ... right ...

David Dear Lord — we ask you at this time to remember Beth, loving wife of — Gordon. We ask You to help her overcome her overwhelming loss of her beloved partner, her rock, her protector, the companion and mainstay of her life. And, although Gordon will remain forever in her heart, nevertheless we ask you to guide Beth to seek out a new and fulfilling future, bringing her new horizons and fresh companions throughout the remaining years of her life. Keep her in health and grant her happiness and give her courage in the years ahead to overcome her loss. Amen.

Connie Amen.

Martin Hear! Hear!

Beth (*softly*) Thank you.

David Well, if you'll excuse me. I have to slip away ... busy time for me ...

Martin Must be.

David Hopefully see you later, Connie. At the carol service.

Connie I'll be there, David. As usual.

David If I can tempt anyone else ... you'd all be welcome.

A slight pause. David looks expectantly at their faces

No? Oh, well. Another year, perhaps? It's usually great fun. (*As he goes*) Happy Christmas, all.

Beth
Martin } (*muttering; rather guiltily*) Happy Christmas.

David exits. Connie follows him

Connie (*off*) I'll see you out, David.

David (*off*) No need, Connie, no need ...

Their voices continue out in the hall for a moment or so

Beth Perhaps we should have said yes. I felt a bit guilty saying no.

Martin We didn't say no. We didn't say anything. Right, let's start unpacking, shall we? You sit down, Mum, leave it all to us. Can you open the back, Ella love?

Beth After I got a free prayer ... (*Sitting*) We should have said we'd go, you know.

Martin Well, you can, Mum. (*Handing Ella the car keys*) There you go. We two'll carry on here. Get things organized won't we, Ella?

Ella goes out without acknowledging Martin

Beth I don't want to go on my own. Be no fun on my own.
Martin Auntie Connie's going. You can go with her.
Beth No. I don't … No, it doesn't matter.
Martin You sit there. Can I get you anything? A drink?
Beth Not at the moment, I've only just had tea.
Martin (*peeling off his jacket*) Right. Get going then. Give Ella a hand. I tell you we've brought mountains of stuff. Presents, booze, food to feed an army … Sit there, you're not to move!

Martin goes out

Beth gets up after a second and, rather restless, moves to the window and gazes out

Oh, what's he driving now, a tank? (*Seeing something*) What's that out there? (*Calling through the window*) Wagstaff? Wagstaff!

Connie enters with a glass of red wine in her hand

Connie I hope you don't mind, Beth, I helped myself to a little drink.
Beth (*still distracted*) Go ahead.
Connie Very quiet, that girl, isn't she?
Beth Probably shy.
Connie Right little chatterbox. You want one?
Beth (*continuing to gaze out of the window*) No.
Connie What's the matter?
Beth I thought I saw something just now. Out there in the bushes. I thought it might have been Wagstaff — come home for Christmas.
Connie I think he's probably gone for good. Cheers!
Beth Cheers!
Connie Well, I have to say. You've made a big hit with David.
Beth Really? Have I?
Connie You know you have. He was all over you. Even had your own private prayer, didn't you? I mean, I think the least he could have done was to include Gordon's son, not to mention his own sister … We never got so much as a mention …
Beth Yes, that was a pity. I think he has trouble remembering names …

Connie He can remember mine. All about you, wasn't it?

Beth Well, don't blame me. I didn't ask him. I never told him what to say, did I?

Connie David's a very vulnerable person, Beth. You shouldn't toy with him if you don't mean it.

Beth I beg your pardon? Toy with him? What on earth are you talking about?

Connie You know what I mean. With his feelings. You can turn a man on a sixpence, you can. Always could do, all the years I've known you.

Beth I don't know what you mean.

Connie You know.

Beth I don't.

Connie You know. (*Significantly*) Mervyn Jacobs.

A pause

Beth If you want my opinion, Connie, I think you've just been listening at too many doors.

Connie What on earth do you mean?

Beth You know.

Connie I have no idea what you're talking about.

Beth You know. (*After a pause; puzzled*) Mervyn Jacobs.

A dignified silence. Both women try to rise above it

Ella enters, laden with bags and boxes. She stops short in the doorway

Beth Kitchen's straight along the hall, love. The door facing you.

Ella goes out to the kitchen

(*To herself, drily*) The house is small enough. No wonder she has trouble reading maps. Who the hell's Mervyn Jacobs when he's at home? Oh, yes, wasn't he the bloke you were keen on, once? What about him?

Connie It's Christmas time, isn't it? We'll say no more about it, shall we?

Beth Please, let's not.

Martin enters with an artificial Christmas tree

Martin Knock-knock! Brought this in from the garage. I'll come and set it up in a minute.

Beth Oh, you shouldn't have dragged that in, Martin.

Martin Why not?

Beth We don't need it. It's just us.

Martin We always have this tree in here. Traditional, isn't it?

Connie Oh, yes, nice to have a tree.

Martin Ever since I was a kid, Dad would set it up. Every Christmas. Wouldn't be the same, would it? All the presents round the base there. Magic.

Beth Well, I've not bought anyone very much this year, I'm afraid.

Connie Nor have I …

Beth … what with one thing and …

Connie No.

Martin We have. You should see that SUV out there. Masses. Mountains.

Connie Oh, you shouldn't have …

Martin Most of them for you, Mum.

Connie Oh.

Beth Oh, Martin, you shouldn't waste your money, you know I ——

Martin I want to, Mum. And I don't consider it wasted. You need a bit of spoiling, especially this Christmas. Listen, I'm going to shift the rest of the stuff into the kitchen, then I'll come back and do the tree. Then we're all having supper in here. Ella's in there now getting that underway …

Beth Is she?

Martin I told you, you're to leave everything to her, Mum. She's cordon bleu trained.

Beth She won't be able to find anything …

Martin Don't worry, once she sets foot in a kitchen, Ella's like a fish in the water. Different woman. She's a bit — shy, you know, at the moment …

Beth Well, if she needs any help, we're just through here. I'm just through here …

Martin No trouble tonight. Tonight's just a cold collation. She plans to start the big stuff tomorrow, wait and see. That's when she plans to really pull the stops out. She's got a chart, you should see it. Planned the entire week right down to the last detail.

Beth Well …

Connie Lovely. Let's leave it to her, then. You know me, I can hardly boil a tea cosy.

Martin Well, you can skivvy, Auntie. You don't mind a spot of skivvying, do you?

Connie (*unenthusiastically*) No.

Martin Then, straight after supper, I'm going to set those garden lights up. Need to do those before we go to bed.

Beth Lights?

Martin The whole place is in darkness out there. We can't have that, can we?

Beth No, Martin, we don't need all that, surely? It was only your father, he ——

Martin Family tradition. What would Dad have to say? The place wouldn't be the same, would it, without the flashing reindeer? Need our flashing reindeer, don't we? Wouldn't be the same without Boris ...

Martin exits

Beth He doesn't need to do that.

Connie He wants to do it.

Beth I always hated all that. It was like Blackpool out there.

Connie It's for his father, Beth. For once, it's not for you. Martin's doing it in memory of his father. Surely you can appreciate that? Surely you can?

Beth remains silent

Now, I'm going to help myself to another little drink, if I may. Then before we have supper, I'm going to have a quick bath.

Beth You do that.

Connie What time are we having it? Supper?

Beth As soon as she's ready, I suppose.

Connie Cold collation. Not sure I like the sound of that.

Beth Cold meat and salad, that's probably all it'll be.

Connie Well, if she's cordon bleu I think the least she could have done is heat something up.

An almighty crash and the sound of breaking glass comes from the kitchen, behind the hatch. Simultaneously, Ella cries out and bursts into tears

Whatever's that? What's happened?

Connie rushes out of the room to investigate

Martin (*off; from the kitchen*) Not on there, I said. (*Yelling*) NOT ON THERE!

Beth Oh, dear God!

Beth hurriedly crosses to the hatch and opens it

Martin (*off*) I told you, didn't I, not to put it on there — I told you —— (*He breaks off, presumably as he sees Beth*)

Ella continues to sob softly in the background

Beth (*surveying the damage through the hatch*) Oh, dear. Everything all right?
Martin (*off*) Yes, yes, fine, Mum. Small accident, we'll cope with it, don't worry.
Connie (*off; as she enters the kitchen, alarmed*) Oh, no! Whatever's happened?
Martin (*off*) It's all right, Auntie. We're dealing with it.
Connie (*off*) What a terrible mess!
Beth (*faintly*) There's a dustpan and brush under the … Oh, God.

Beth gives up and closes the hatch

(*Muttering*) I think I am going to need a drink at this rate.

She starts to randomly tidy the room, straightening a chair here, an ornament there

Oh, I feel like a spare sock on a one-legged sailor.

Another clatter is heard coming from the kitchen

(*Reacting*) Oh, I can't stand it a minute longer, I … (*She heads determinedly for the door*)

Martin enters and nearly collides with Beth. He is holding an opened can of beer which he occasionally quaffs from

Martin Whoops! Now, Mum, where do you think you're going? Sit down!
Beth I can't bear this, I feel I'm under house arrest. I need to be doing something, Martin.
Martin I told you there's nothing for you to do.
Beth It's Christmas! All this sitting down's not good for me, it feels unnatural.

Martin All in hand.

Beth Sounds like it.

Martin Slight accident, that's all. Nothing serious.

Beth Sounded as if she'd dropped the china cabinet.

Martin Nothing that can't be replaced. Now then — (*turning his attention to the Christmas tree*) I'll just set this up. Plug it in. Away we go.

Under the next, Martin erects the tree, standing it in the corner of the room. It is one of those floor-standing, artificial trees with a detachable base on which the branches hinge for packing purposes. The lights have been previously attached and wired to the branches. It all requires a certain amount of straightening and artistic branch 'grooming' which Martin does in due course. Beth watches him

You all right there, Mum? Can I get you anything?

Beth No, thanks, Martin. Not at the moment.

A pause. Beth watches Martin

I am going to be allowed to go to the toilet on my own, I hope?

Martin Only if you put your hand up.

Beth So long as I know.

Martin That's the trouble with you. Can't bear sitting still, can you? Not for a minute. Spent your life running after Dad and me. Time you sat down, isn't it?

Beth I'm not used to sitting down. I'm used to being on my feet. Doing things.

Martin There's nothing to do, I keep saying …

Beth There's masses to do, Martin. I mean, you three can't … I mean, how can you possibly …? I mean, it's Christmas Eve … this time of year I'm usually rushed off my feet. Wrapping and stuffing things … hanging the holly. (*Unhappily*) There's masses …

Connie looks in, holding a re-filled wine glass

Connie That's all cleaned up in there, anyway. Down on my hands and knees as usual. Just going up for a quick bath, get changed. (*Indicating her glass*) Oh, I helped myself, I hope you don't mind, Beth.

Beth Help yourself.

Connie Oh, that looks nice, Martin.

Martin It will do. Eventually.

Connie (*as she goes*) Lovely and Christmassy.

Connie goes out

Beth I hope she's not going to get pissed again, like she did last year.
Martin I'll keep an eye on her, don't worry.
Beth Trying to ride the flashing reindeer. That really had your dad going.
Martin Bloody hell, yes. Burnt her legs, didn't she?
Beth That's not all she burnt. I got through that much Savlon ...
Martin (*now absorbed*) How about you? Fancy a drink?
Beth No. I'll wait 'til supper.

The sound of a dropping saucepan lid is heard from the kitchen, behind the hatch. Beth and Martin register this but then choose not to comment

You don't need to go to all this trouble, Martin, you really don't. Not just for me.
Martin (*intent on his task*) Yes, I do.
Beth Not just for me.
Martin For me as well. I need to do it for me. And for Dad. He'd expect it.
Beth I don't think he would. Why do you feel he'd expect it?
Martin He just would. I know he would.
Beth Why?
Martin I'm his son.
Beth And?
Martin He took care of you, didn't he? All your married life. All thirty-whatever years of it ...
Beth Thirty-three.
Martin Devoted to you. Like you were to him. He looked after you, saw you right, gave us a home. Worked his socks off, didn't he? We never wanted for nothing, not really. He did everything a man should do.
Beth (*gently*) I looked after him, too. I did a little bit as well, Martin.
Martin No, but he was, like, the provider, wasn't he? Once you'd stopped work, when you had me — and then Karen — nursing her, 'til she ... Dad was the sole provider, wasn't he? Now it's fallen to me. I know I could never be quite what he was for you — no way — I mean, you two were that close, weren't you? — Friends of mine they used to say you and Dad, you were the perfect couple ...
Beth We had our moments ...
Martin Let's face it, you never argued, did you? All the time I was growing up, I never once heard a cross word between you. Lads at

school, they said their mums and dads used to go at it like hammer and tongs sometimes.

Beth No, we never argued. I sometimes didn't agree with him but I never argued with him ...

Martin Never an angry word here ...

Beth ... there was no point, really ...

Martin ... I could never live up to that ...

Beth ... he never listened to me ...

Martin ... never. You heard me in there. Yelling at Ella. Yelling at her. Dad would never have done that, would he?

Beth No, your dad never yelled.

Martin I made her cry, didn't I, you heard me. That's terrible.

Beth Yes, well, she's over it now, isn't she?

Martin I yelled at her in the car coming here, as well ... I don't know what comes over me ...

Beth Well, sometimes, you know it's good to have a good yell ...

Martin Not when it makes someone cry, it isn't.

Beth Well, occasionally women need a good cry, you know. They enjoy it, Martin. Some women. Your Auntie Connie does. She loves a good cry.

Martin You don't cry. I've never seen you cry, Mum.

Beth No. I don't cry very much. I didn't think I'd cry at the funeral, but I did. Surprised me. Oh, and I cried when Karen finally went ... but ... All I'm saying is that some women, you know, they weep buckets. They're always bursting into tears. Your Auntie Connie cries at TV adverts. Maybe Ella's one of those. You never know.

Martin Most of the women I've gone out with start crying sooner or later.

Beth You've not had a lot of luck with your women, have you?

A pause. Another clatter is heard from the kitchen which again they both register and then choose to ignore

Martin (*finishing with the tree*) Right, that's it, that'll do. Plug it in, let's have a look at it.

Beth Oh, well done. That looks lovely, Martin.

Martin (*plugging the lights into a wall socket*) And — the moment of truth! (*He switches it on. Nothing happens*) Typical.

Beth Not working?

Martin No.

Beth Probably just a bulb.

Martin Typical. (*He starts tightening each bulb separately, working his way round the tree*)

Beth I don't know why they make them like that, do you? I can't see the point, can you? One bulb goes out, they all go out. Why do they make them like that, do you know? I mean, if they all go out, how's anyone supposed to know which one of them it is that's just gone out. Why do they make them like that, do you suppose?

Martin (*he hasn't the foggiest*) Well, they design it ... in series — you know, in phase ... because of electrical resistance, you know ... safety ... optimum loading and so on ...

Beth I mean, if one bulb goes in here, they don't go out all over the house as well, do they? Your dad explained it to me once but I couldn't follow it. Not after the first ten minutes, anyway.

Another crash is heard from the kitchen

Martin No, I think it may be the plug. I'll just fetch the toolbox.
Beth Under the stairs, where it usually is.

Martin goes out

More sounds are heard from the kitchen. This time there are a series of thumps, as of someone hitting a stove with their hand. Beth cautiously moves to open the hatch. As she opens it, the thumps grow louder. Ella's effortful grunts are also heard

You all right there, love?

The thumping continues

If you're trying to get that oven door open — a little tip — you need just to lift it slightly first, love.

More thumping

No, you just have to lift it first. It's a safety feature. Just lift it — that's it.

The thumping stops

It's a stupid stove. My husband insisted we got one. Full of these safety features, it's hopeless. Drives you mad. Oh, look, warm bread, how lovely. I love warm bread. If you need a hand, just give a yell, won't you?

Beth closes the hatch

As she does so, Martin returns with a large toolbox

Martin Knock-knock! Back again!
Beth I was just seeing she was all right.
Martin She's all right. I've seen her cook up a three course dinner for ten. No hassle.
Beth Really?
Martin Didn't even break sweat. (*He sits by the tree and starts to unscrew the plug*)
Beth She seemed to be having trouble getting the oven open ... Still, that stove, it's got a mind of its own.
Martin Ella's more used to industrial stuff, you know.
Beth Yes?
Martin You know. Big industrial ranges.
Beth Well, I'd better lay the table. At least I can do that.

During the following, Beth goes to the sideboard and locates cutlery, mats, a cruet and two new Christmas candles. She starts to lay up the table for four

What does Ella do exactly? You did tell me, didn't you?
Martin Chef. She ran her own restaurant for a bit.
Beth Really?
Martin That's how we first met, actually. Went there to eat couple of times. Only unfortunately it closed. Nothing to do with her, mind you.
Beth No ...
Martin Not her fault, at all. Dodgy partner. He ran off with the money.
Beth Oh, dear ...
Martin So she's, like, between restaurants, you know. Freelancing. Mind you, she's no shortage of offers. There's demand for her. All around the Dorchester area, you know. She's a bit special, really. In the catering world. Special ...
Beth You're fond of her then?
Martin Oh, yes. She's — (*He concentrates on the plug for a second*) Come on, come on, you little ... (*He pauses*) She's — Ella's — just amazing. (*Shaking his head at the memory*) Poetry. You've no idea. I couldn't begin to tell you, Mum. Not without making you blush. You know.
Beth I'm pleased for you, son. Are we having pudding, do you know? I don't know whether we need spoons and forks ...
Martin (*studying the plug*) Oh, there we are! There we are. Cause of the trouble. Loose wire.

Beth Oh, well done.
Martin Pulled loose, that's all.
Beth Can you fix it?
Martin No problem. (*He reassembles the plug*)

Ella opens the kitchen hatchway

Beth Is it ready, then? Oh, wonderful ...

Ella pushes two plates through the hatch. They contain a quite pleasantly presented, modest-sized salad concoction, vertically presented

I'll take them from here, love, I'll take them.
Martin Hey, I'm starving.
Beth Doesn't this look amazing? (*To Ella; calling*) Incidentally, is there a pudding, love? Only I was wondering to lay spoons and ... (*Getting little apparent response*) ... no, probably not.

Beth takes the first two plates to the table

(*As she does so, to Martin; quietly*) By the way, I've put you both in our room.
Martin Right.
Beth I thought you'd prefer it in the double.
Martin (*giving a thumbs-up*) Thanks, Mum.

Connie enters. She is transformed: clothes, hair, make-up

Beth Well, look at you!
Martin Auntie's smelt the food!
Beth (*putting the plates on the table*) All dressed for dinner?
Connie Well, I thought I'd make the effort, you know ... and with me going on later ...
Beth Oh, yes. Look at this, Connie, doesn't it look delicious?

Ella passes two more plates through the hatch. Beth takes them

Connie (*looking at the food; rather dubiously*) Yes ...
Beth Whoops, this one's rather toppled over. I'll have to have this one.
Martin (*completing his plug*) That's done it!
Beth Would you mind bringing the white wine from the fridge, Ella? If you wouldn't mind?

Ella closes the hatch

Oh, now glasses, we need glasses. Connie, would you mind? In the cupboard there. We need four. We'd all like a drop of white wine with our dinner, wouldn't we?

Connie (*getting out the wine glasses*) I'll stick with the red.

Beth Suit yourself. (*Opening the hatch*) Ella, could you bring the red through as well, please — oh, she's gone.

Martin I'll get it.

Martin goes out with the toolbox. He hasn't yet switched on the Christmas tree lights

Connie That bath water was a bit tepid, you know, Beth.

Beth Oh, dear. Well, nobody's had one recently. It's the immersion probably, playing up again. I'll have to get the plumber. Don't ask me. Gordon was the only one who understood it. It's full of over-ride features.

Ella enters, rather flushed from her labours, carrying the white wine and a covered basket of warm bread

Doesn't this all look lovely? Bravo!

Beth gives Ella a little round of applause which Ella hardly acknowledges

Now, how are we all going to sit? I'll be here, as always. (*Sitting at one end of the table*) Ella, would you like to sit here, love? (*Indicating to her right*) Connie, you go here and — Martin can go at the end. In his dad's place.

Connie Man of the house.

Beth Yes. Now you must tell me how you do this, Ella. I can never get it looking like this ...

Connie It looks quite simple, really ...

Beth I can never get mine to stand up. It's a great art, I imagine? Getting it to stand up? (*Pouring wine for herself and Ella*) It looks delicious, don't you think, Connie?

Silence

(*Calling*) Come on Martin, where are you? We want to eat! We're all starving hungry in here!

Connie Well, I hope this keeps us going. It needs to last us through 'til breakfast, doesn't it?

Martin enters with a bottle of red wine

Martin Sorry. Had to open a fresh bottle, that one was practically empty.

Connie Well, if we're still hungry after this, we'll just have fill up on sweet. I presume there's a sweet?

Beth — er …

Connie Martin?

Martin — er … I'm not sure.

Beth Well, this looks very filling, anyway. We don't need too much, do we? Spoil our appetite for tomorrow, won't it? Now, do sit down, we're all dying to start.

Connie Try not to eat it all at once.

Martin Now, who's this red for? Just for you is it, Auntie Connie? May I?

Connie Thank you.

Beth I've put you up that end, Martin, in your — where your dad used to sit …

Connie Man of the house.

Martin Right. Oh, we haven't got the Christmas tree, have we? Just a tick. (*He goes to the tree*) We must have the lights. And — let there be light.

Martin clicks the wall switch. There is a small bang and all the lights go out. They are now lit only with the residual street light glow from the window

Beth } Oh, no!
Connie } What's happened?

Martin Whoops! Sorry about that, ladies! Technical fault.

Beth It's the fuse.

Martin Yes, it's probably the fuse. Don't panic, girls. I'll find the fuse box. Fix it in no time.

Beth Under the stairs. I'll go, if you like.

Martin No I'll go, I'll do it. No sweat. I'm a dab hand with fuses. If I can find my way.

Beth Martin, have your supper first. Tell you what, we can light the candles, can't we?

Martin Oh yes, why not? Dinner by candlelight. Very romantic.

Beth Anyone got a light?

Martin I've got one. I've got one here. If I can find my way.

Martin gropes his way back to the table

Connie Oooh!
Martin Sorry, Auntie Connie. Now then. Here we go. (*He lights one of the candles*)

The candle gives sufficient light to reveal, at the other end of the table in the seat reserved for him, the figure of Gordon

Beth, who appears to be the only one of them who can see her late husband, rises in alarm

Beth Oh, my God! It's him!
Martin Mum! What is it, Mum?
Connie Beth, what's the matter with you?

Ella looks alarmed. Beth sways for a moment and swoons to the floor in a heap. Ella gives a small scream

Martin } Mum!
Connie ⌡ Catch her!

They gather round Beth in consternation as Gordon remains seated in a ghostly light

The Lights fade to Black-out

ACT II

The same. An hour or so later

The table has been cleared, the sofa bed has been made up and although the Christmas tree remains unlit, the main lights have been restored. The room is now lit by a single table lamp standing on a side table next to the sofa, now serving as a temporary bedside light. Outside in the garden, behind the closed curtains and thus not too noticeable at present, a light pulses on and off, evidence that the illuminated reindeer is now functioning

Beth, in her nightclothes, is sitting up in the sofa bed, staring at the corner of the room where Gordon previously materialized and of whom there is currently no sign

Beth (*softly; rather nervously*) … Don't you dare … don't you bloody dare come back to haunt me, do you hear? Gordon? I know you're there …

Martin, who is still dressed, appears silently in the doorway, unseen by Beth

I can see you, you know … I know you're there … I know there's someone here. I know there is …

Martin (*tentatively*) Knock-knock …

Beth (*startled*) Oh, God! Martin! (*Gently*) Listen, love, try not to do that too much, would you?

Martin How do you mean?

Beth All that "knock-knock" business …

Martin Sorry. I didn't realize …

Beth It's just a tiny little bit irritating, love. That's all. Either knock on the door properly or come into the room. One or the other.

Martin Right. Dad always used to do it, didn't he?

Beth Yes, he did.

Martin Sorry. You all right then, Mum?

Beth Yes, yes. Still a little — shook up … you know …

Martin You sure you won't take something?

Beth No, no ... I'm fine now ...

Martin Ella's got some sleeping pills. She says you're welcome to one of those, if you ...

Beth No, no. You know me and pills. Never take them unless there's an emergency.

Martin I think that was an emergency. Fainting like that. I've never known you to ——

Beth Well, I'm over it now.

Martin If you're sure.

Beth I'm fine, Martin, you're not to worry about me, do you hear? It's very sweet of you, but ... go on upstairs to bed now. Ella will be wondering where you are ——

Martin No, well I didn't want to disturb her. Let her get to sleep. She's taken a couple of pills. Bit shaken up by all of this, you know.

Beth Sleeping pills? Ella takes sleeping pills?

Martin Well, relaxants, you know. Now and then. To relax her. Things tonight made her a bit tense ... not just the — you know — apparition ... I think she was a bit hurt that no one ate much of the dinner ...

Beth I was lying there flat on my back in the middle of the floor, Martin, I was hardly going to tuck into a pile of mixed salad, was I?

Martin No, no. No one's to blame. I ate it. I ate two and a half of them, anyway, but it wasn't the same. She was just, you know, a bit hurt, you know ...

Beth It was all right for her. She wasn't the one who saw something, was she?

Martin You really ... saw ... thought you saw ... Dad? You saw him? ...

Beth I thought I did. Clear as day. Sitting there in his own chair, you know. Just like he used to. With his arms folded, waiting for his dinner. It was weird ... I could have sworn he ... really weird.

Martin I think you should have a check-up, Mum.

Beth Possibly.

Martin In the New Year. They say grief, you know, like you've got, can have profound side effects, trick the mind into ... I'm going to try, Mum. It'll be difficult but — I'll try to take his place. Make up the difference.

Beth You don't need to do that, Martin. I've said.

Martin But there must be such a hole in your life now. Such a gap where Dad used to be. I mean, it's like you've lost a whole half of you. I know you're very clever at hiding things, always have been, but I can see how you're feeling.

Beth It'll heal over. Eventually. Life goes on. Hopefully. (*She pauses slightly*) Auntie Connie back, is she?

Martin Not yet. I was half waiting up for her ...

Beth What time is it?

Martin (*consulting his watch*) Just gone twenty to two ... Oh. Happy Christmas, by the way ...

Beth Happy Christmas. That's odd. She should be back by now. Carol service doesn't go on for two hours, surely ... Maybe she's — gone on ...

Martin Where's she gone on to after a midnight service? Run off with the vicar, has she?

Beth Now you mention it ...

Martin What?

Beth ... nothing.

Martin I hope she's all right. She was well away before she went, wasn't she?

Beth She was ...

Martin (*looking to the ceiling*) Well, I think Ella must be asleep, I'd better get up there. I left the reindeer on by the way. In the front garden. Hope it won't keep you awake.

Beth Can't you switch it off?

Martin I've tried. But there's a timer. Which must have an over-ride, somewhere, but I can't seem to figure it out. Full of safety features.

Beth Well, it can't keep flashing on and off all night.

Martin The only solution is to take the whole thing down again ... and after the trouble it took to ... I'll sort it out in the morning, Mum, don't worry ...

Beth It'll keep people awake though. We'll get complaints.

Martin Yes, the bloke next door did pop round ...

Beth What, Bill Chambers ...?

Martin He was very pleasant, considering. It was just his kids were waking up every ten minutes apparently, thinking Santa'd arrived ... I hope it won't disturb you.

Beth It might disturb you two. You're just above here. It's right outside your window.

Martin No, that's all right. Ella has a sleep mask.

Beth Sleep mask?

Martin She has a — touch of insomnia. Occasionally. Anyway, I managed to get these lights on again. Fixed the fuse.

Beth (*gently*) Yes, you did, Son. With a little bit of help from me.

There is a loud knock on the front door. The doorbell rings simultaneously. Beth and Martin jump

God! That'll be her! Auntie Connie!

Beth Or more neighbours.

Martin (*hurrying out*) I hope to God she hasn't woken Ella ...

More knocking

I'll deal with it, Mum. (*Calling*) Coming, I'm coming ...

Martin goes out

Beth (*sighing*) Oh, dear ... I'm really so tired ...

Beth lies back. Voices can be heard outside in the hall. Amidst this, Connie's drunken groans and slurred protests can also be heard

Man (*off*) Good evening, sir. Can you confirm this lady lives here?
Martin (*off*) Oh, my God! What's happened to her?
Man (*off*) Can you verify this is her current address? She's not sure.
Martin (*off*) Oh, yes, that's my Auntie Connie. What's happened to her? What's she done?
Man (*off*) Your Auntie Connie's just assaulted this officer.
Woman (*off*) When apprehended as she was attempting to climb the statue in the town square ——
Martin (*off*) Oh, my God!
Woman (*off*) — trying to get on the horse. She's very lucky we don't press charges.
Man (*off*) I should put Auntie to bed, if I were you. She's lucky not to be locked up.

Ella can be heard coming down the stairs

Ella (*off*) Martin? What's happening? What the hell's going on? What the bloody hell's happening?
Man (*off*) Hallo, who's this then, your fairy godmother?
Woman (*off*) Here! Will you take her from me, dear? Watch yourself, she scratches.
Ella (*off*) I don't want her. Don't give her to me! Why don't you take her, Martin! She's your bloody auntie!
Martin (*off*) Ella! Ella! Ella! Please! I will, I'll take her in a minute, love.
Man (*off*) She can just consider herself lucky we're too busy looking after serious drunks to bother with her. Take my tip, you'll put her to bed to sleep it off. You tell her in the morning she's old enough to know better and she ought to be ashamed of herself. Good night to you.

Martin (*off*) Thank you very much. Merry Christmas.

The door closes. Connie continues her noises

Wait there, Ella! Just one second. I'm just going to tell Mum what's happened. Then I'll come and help you with her.
Ella (*off*) I can't hold her on my own, Martin! Hurry up!
Beth (*sometime during the above, lying back; wearily*) What's everyone doing? What's going on? What the hell's going on?

Martin enters

Martin Knock-kno —— (*Remembering*) Sorry, Mum …
Beth (*wearily*) Yes?
Martin Not asleep, are you?
Beth No …
Martin Only, in case you were wondering, it was only the police.
Beth (*sitting up, alarmed*) The what?
Martin They just brought Auntie Connie back. She's a bit under the … you know …
Beth (*making as if to get out of bed*) Oh, God …
Martin No! No! Mum! Ella's seeing her into bed. You stay there, we're taking care of it, it's all under control.
Beth What was she doing?
Martin Ella? She'd just got off to sleep.
Beth No, Connie. What was Connie doing for heaven's sake?
Martin Apparently, she was trying to climb the statue …
Beth The statue? What statue?
Martin The one in the town square. The one with the bloke on the horse. Oliver Cromwell, isn't it?
Beth The Duke of Wellington …
Martin The good news is that they're not going to charge her …
Beth They're not?
Martin They said they were far too busy looking after serious drunks to bother with her and that she should go to bed and sleep it off and that she was old enough to know better at her age and she ought to be ashamed of herself.
Beth Well, if you need any help with her, let me know …
Martin No, she's calm now. She put up a bit of a fight, they said. Scratched the policewoman … Why don't you switch off the light, Mum? Try and get a bit of sleep. You'll need it. Busy day tomorrow, eh?
Beth Yes, yes. I'll try.

Martin Right. I'll go up, then. Give Ella a hand. You need anything?
Beth Just a bit of quiet, would be nice.
Martin Well, there shouldn't be any more excitements. 'Night then, Mum.
Beth Good night, Martin.
Martin Want me to turn the light out for you?
Beth No, I'll do it. Martin, would you make sure, before you go up that everything else is turned off, please?
Martin Will do, Mum. 'Night, 'night.
Beth 'Night.

Martin goes out

Beth, on her own again, stares around the room nervously

You're still here, Gordon, I can sense you. I know you are. I don't want to see you again, do you hear me? They say if you don't want to see ghosts, they don't appear. Well, I don't want to see you, d'you hear? I'm turning this light off now. And I'm going to sleep. All right? (*Placing her hand on the light switch*) One ... two ... three ...

Beth's bedside light goes off. The room is comparatively darker, however the effect of the flashing lights through the window gets correspondingly brighter

Oh, my God. It's like bloody Las Vegas! Still, at least I can see. I can see whether you're here or not.

She listens to the silence for a moment

Right, then. Nothing. All quiet!

Suddenly the kitchen hatch bursts open and a shaft of light illuminates the room

(*Alarmed*) Oh!

Martin's head appears through the hatch

Martin (*whispering*) Sorry to startle you, Mum!
Beth What?
Martin She left the oven on.
Beth What?
Martin Ella. She went and left the oven on.
Beth Did she?

Martin Left it on low. Just turned it off. She's more used to industrial ones, you know. I'm going up now.
Beth Good.
Martin 'Night, then, Mum.
Beth 'Night.

Martin closes the hatch

Oh, sleep. Blessed sleep ...

Silence. The lights flash on and off for a moment or two. A faint scratching sound comes from the hatch doorway in the kitchen

What's that?

Beth listens. The scratching sound occurs again, louder this time

Sounds like — Wagstaff? Wagstaff ... (*She clambers out of bed*) Wagstaff! (*She opens the hatch; tentatively*) Wagstaff? Nothing ... I'm being haunted by the cat now.

Beth closes the hatch doors and makes to return to bed

Gordon is again sitting at the table in his corner chair, facing her

(*Seeing him and clutching her heart*) Aaah!
Gordon (*cheerily*) Knock-knock.
Beth (*drawing back*) Gordon? Is that you? Is that really you?
Gordon It is indeed. (*Jovially*) And who else did you expect to find in your bedroom at this time of night, may I ask?
Beth (*starting to lose her grip slightly*) It can't really be you ... I mean, it can't be ... I mean, I sat by your bed when you — while you were ...
Gordon While I was departing, yes, I do recall ...
Beth And then we took you up to the ... up to the ...
Gordon Crematorium, yes.
Beth And then we ... they ... they ...
Gordon Cremated me, yes ...
Beth And then I took your ... then I took your ...
Gordon My ashes, yes.
Beth And I scatt — I scatt — I scatt ...
Gordon Scattered them, yes, in the park, didn't you? In accordance with my final wishes. The Victoria Park. Though I did specify the

other end, Beth, you know, the south west end, by the lake. That north east end you chose, they did tend to blow back a bit into the kiddies' playground which I did feel was a little unhygienic ...

Beth (*weakly*) I'm sorry, it was very windy, I'm sorry ... I was aiming for the rose beds. I know how you liked roses ...

Gordon No, well, you did your best. You can't do better than your best. I always say that of you, Beth, you're always trying if not quite succeeding. You may occasionally fall a whisker short of perfection, but I can never fault you for trying. And that, when the chips are down, is what counts.

Beth Gordon, why have you come back? What are you doing here? What have I done? Why have you come back to haunt me?

Gordon I've not come back to haunt you, certainly not ...

Beth ... because I don't know what more I could have done ...

Gordon ... I'm back to keep an eye on you. Make sure you're coping without me.

Beth I can cope, don't worry about me.

Gordon Now where have I heard that before? "I can manage, Gordon, don't worry, I can manage." And the next minute, where are we? All sixes and sevens ... Or in your case, as often as not, sevens and eights, eh?

Beth Listen, Gordon, I can't deal with this.

Gordon Ah well, there, you see. A case in point. There's one problem you can't deal with for a kick off ... now who says you don't need me here?

Beth Yes but you're the problem, Gordon. Please go away.

Gordon I can't do that, Beth. I'm sorry.

Beth You can't?

Gordon No, this is an official visit, you see. Authorized as the result of formal request.

Beth Who by?

Gordon I'm afraid I'm not at liberty to disclose that information.

Beth You're not?

Gordon I'm under oath. As a result of one or two small services I have been able to render, I have been granted official dispensation.

Beth Small services? What small services?

Gordon Again, I regret I'm unable to disclose that. Suffice it to say that, following my demise, when I arrived there, the place was little short of a shambles, as my father would have said. Since I arrived, I'm pleased to report that systems are gradually being put into place. I'm introducing flow charts, comparison graphs and optimum attainment targets like there's no tomorrow — which as it happens up there, there isn't. By the time you get there, which I trust will be a little while yet,

Beth, everything will be operating as smooth as clockwork. And not before time. But you'll be familiar with all this, Beth. I don't need to tell you, do I? You know me ...

Beth Yes, I know you, Gordon. Only too well.

Gordon Like a red rag to a bull for me, all that.

A door slams upstairs. They both look up, momentarily

Beth You're still the same, Gordon. You haven't changed.

Gordon Oh, no, just the same. Take more than a — slight change of circumstances — to alter me. (*Smiling*) Frankly, they were simply amazed. Gobsmacked.

Beth Who were?

Gordon The — persons concerned. I can't reveal their identities. But they were amazed. "Heavens above, Mr Timms, I don't know how we've managed without you all these years." I tell you, they were open-mouthed. Jaws to their knees. I told them, all it takes is a fresh eye. I mean, the majority of the procedures there were outdated, some of them were downright dangerous.

Beth Oh, dear.

Gordon I told them that. I didn't mince words, I was perfectly blunt with them.

Beth I bet.

Gordon But don't you worry, Beth, I'm setting them straight. Little by little.

Beth Well done.

Gordon Confidentially, *entre nous*, I think the problem goes higher. Much higher. I'll sort that out next. Yes, they're glad of me. (*After a slight, self-congratulatory pause*) Just like old times this, isn't it?

A bump is heard from the bedroom upstairs

Beth Yes ...

Gordon Me chattering away. You listening agog.

Beth Yes ...

Gordon How it always used to be, eh?

Beth Yes ...

Gordon You know, I don't mind saying, I'm quite looking forward to getting back into the swing of things, you know.

Beth Where?

Gordon Here.

Beth You're planning on staying?

Gordon Oh, yes.

Beth How long for?

Gordon Well, just until.

Beth Until when?

Gordon Just until. (*He considers*) Listen, Beth, I just want to say something to you.

Beth Oh, yes? Something else?

Gordon It's this. Now, as I'm sure you recall, due to circumstances beyond my personal control, I underwent a work-related accident in my place of employment ... from which I subsequently was forced to retire. Now, during those final few weeks in the hospital and here at home, I'm aware that my ill health prevented me from putting into place adequate safeguards and correct procedures sufficient to guarantee your future well-being and livelihood ...

Beth I've got the pension ...

Gordon Yes, allow me to ——

Beth ... and the insurance ...

Gordon ... allow me to ...

Beth I had the compensation, too. From Twistleton's. They paid up ...

Gordon ... Beth ...

Beth ... eventually, they did.

Gordon ... Beth. Would you allow me to finish, please? Would you mind?

Beth (*meekly*) Sorry.

Gordon Never quite hear me through, do you? Never listen to the end of a sentence, do you?

Beth I never know when you've got there.

Gordon I'm not talking about the money, love. I know there's enough money. Well, there should be, for your needs. I mean, there's never enough money but ... No, what I'm talking about is how you manage it. How you manage the money, do you see? Now that was always left to me, wasn't it?

Beth Only because you wanted to, I could probably have ——

Gordon Beth, come on, come on, be fair. Be honest, now. Not what you'd term a financial brain, is it, yours? Could you, hand on heart, could you possibly have dealt with all that side for thirty-three years? Investments? Variable rates of interest? The fluctuating pound? Mortgage rates? Retail price index. No, you left it to Gordon, didn't you? Quite sensibly. In the same way, be fair, fair do's, I left certain things to you. When you wanted to re-decorate, say, the bedroom, did I interfere in any way? No, I did not. Never said a word. When we changed this carpet in here ...

Beth You did with the bathroom. You insisted ——

Gordon Well, the bathroom, yes. That's my area. That's plumbing. Tiling and grouting and so on ...

Beth You didn't do that yourself. We got the plumber in ...

Gordon And who, may I enquire, supervised him? Virtually stood over the man while he was doing it?

Beth I was left with all the boring bits, wasn't I? Toilet roll holders and soap dishes ...

Gordon Now, now, now, now ...

Beth ... lavatory brushes ... I could have chosen the tiles.

Gordon What is there to choose with tiles? White is white, isn't it?

Beth Why do they always need to be white?

Gordon All bathroom tiles are white!

Beth (*muttering*) I'd have liked pink. Greyish pink.

Gordon (*scornfully*) Greyish pink? Come on, how could you ever tell they were clean?

Beth I'd have known.

Gordon Well, I wouldn't.

Beth You'd never have cleaned them.

Gordon (*after a slight pause*) I'm not sure I'm liking the sound of this, Beth. This sounds like the beginnings of an argument, if you ask me ...

Beth Not really, I'm just saying ——

Gordon Thirty-three years and never a cross word and then hey presto, I'm out of the house for a couple of weeks and when I come back there's a palace revolution underway. Dear me! Things certainly do need organizing, don't they? Dear, oh dear!

Another bump is heard coming from upstairs

Martin (*off; despairing*) Well, what *do* you want from me, for God's sake?

Beth You say this is an official visit?

Gordon It has been authorized, yes.

Beth As a result of a formal request, you said?

Gordon That is correct.

Beth Where did the request come from, then?

Gordon I'm afraid I'm not at liberty to ——

Beth To disclose that information. Well, I think I have a right to know, Gordon. I mean, it was a request made on my behalf. Did it come from you?

Gordon I'm not saying, Beth, I'm not saying. My lips are sealed.

Beth Oh, when you get like this, you can be so annoying, Gordon. I could strangle you, you know, if you weren't already dead. (*She pauses*) You're not telling me? (*She pauses*) All right. See if I care.

Gordon (*after a pause*) I'll simply say ... your beloved partner ...
your rock ... your protector ... the companion and mainstay of your
life ...

Beth (*realizing*) Oh. But it wasn't me who said that.

Gordon It was said on your behalf. By an intermediary. You approved
it.

Beth I never knew he was going to say that ...

Gordon Nonetheless it caught someone's attention ...

Beth Who? Oh, you mean ...

Gordon Well, possibly not. I believed the request was intercepted at
committee level. They did feel, though, it warranted immediate action.
They generously allowed me to step down temporarily from my duties
there and here I am.

Beth Listen, I'm trying to tell you, Gordon. I'm all right. I had the
dreadful shock of losing you and for a week or two I was — I was
beside myself with grief, I admit it ... But I'm gradually getting over
it, love ... I'm coming to terms with it, you see. With being alone.
Listen, I hate to say this to your face, it sounds so terrible, but I really
don't need you, Gordon, not any more ... I'm very sorry, but I don't.
(*She pauses for breath*)

Gordon (*calmly*) If you could only hear yourself, Beth. Now it's late
and you're tired, and you're in an emotional state ...

Beth (*excitedly*) Of course I'm in an emotional state, who wouldn't
be in an emotional state? I'm holding this conversation with my late
husband, aren't I ...?

Gordon Now, Beth, calmly, old girl ...

Beth ... who still won't listen to me, even when he's dead.

Gordon (*moving to Beth slightly*) Lie down now, lie down!

Beth (*drawing back and sitting on the bed*) Don't you touch me!

Gordon Don't worry, I can't touch you, we're on different astral planes,
Beth ...

Beth Thank God for that ...

Gordon My hand would pass right through you. Now lie down, close
your eyes.

Beth does so, reluctantly

We can't have this, can we? Disagreements? Thirty-three years and
never a cross word between us, was there? Was there?

Beth No. Not out loud, anyway.

Gordon Oh, come on, old girl. I won't hear talk like that. Bite your
tongue, woman! You know, when I was alive, I told everyone that I
had married the perfect wife. Couldn't fault her. In my opinion, we

had the perfect marriage. And I hoped that she felt the same. In fact, I know she did. It was a true meeting of two minds and, on occasions, two bodies.

Beth On occasions ...

Gordon Now I'm telling them all over again up there. You were perfection, Beth. I couldn't have asked for better. If I was to have my life over, I would not have altered a single nanosecond. Nary a one ...

Beth (*sleepily*) That's nice, Gordon. I'm very happy for you. (*She yawns*)

Gordon That's it, why don't you get some shut-eye, old girl? You've had a busy day, haven't you?

Beth You can say that again.

Gordon I'll leave you now. I'll be back in the morning, don't worry.

Beth Oh. Will you?

Gordon 'Nighty-night, then.

Beth Gordon ...

Gordon Yes.

Beth Have you seen Wagstaff at all? Do you know if he's still alive?

Gordon Oh, no. I'm afraid, once again, can't reveal ...

Beth I couldn't bear to think of him still alive, injured or trapped somewhere ... I just wanted to check he wasn't with you ...

Gordon Oh, no, he wouldn't be with me ... No. Cats go — cats go elsewhere.

Beth To another astral plane ...?

Gordon If you like ...

Beth (*with her eyes closed, smiling*) Pussy cat heaven ...

Gordon (*withdrawing to a dark corner of the room*) Possibly. Or knowing that cat ... somewhere completely other.

From upstairs we hear the sound of Ella crying, followed by heavy footsteps across the floor and the slamming of a door

Martin (*off*) Oh, God, no — no — *no!*

Beth sits up, wide awake

As she does so, Gordon steps back into the far corner of the room and vanishes

Beth Now what? Oh, what a night!

Martin arrives in the doorway. He is still dressed but in his stockinged feet. He carries his shoes

Martin Knock-knock!

Beth (*very sharply, for her*) Yes? What is it now?

Martin Sorry, Mum.

Beth Sorry, love.

Martin You weren't asleep, were you?

Beth No. I was talking to — to ... (*looking to where Gordon had been*) just talking to myself.

Martin Oh. First sign of madness, isn't it?

Beth Possibly. What is it, love? What's the problem, then?

Martin It's — er ... well ... She's ... she's ...

Beth A problem, is it? With Ella?

Martin Ella? Oh, no, that's all fine. You know, couldn't be better — whoarr!

Beth (*a bit puzzled*) Good. I'm pleased to hear it. What's that there?

Martin Sorry?

Beth On your shoes?

Martin Oh, yes. That's why I came down. Auntie Connie's been sick on the landing ...

Beth (*falling back on the bed again*) Oh, for God's sake! Happy Christmas!

Martin (*rather bemused*) Happy Christmas!

The Lights fade to Black-out

SCENE 2

The same. Christmas Day, around midday

The sofa bed is re-assembled. The presents, mostly unopened, are still piled up under the unlit Christmas tree

Beth has dressed and is now sitting on her own in the middle of the sofa. Unsurprisingly, she looks pale and drawn from lack of sleep. She is surrounded by scraps of wrapping paper from a present she has recently opened. The present itself, a stole which clashes alarmingly with the outfit she now wears, is draped, forgotten, around her shoulders

The TV is on. The jolliest of Christmas programmes carries on inappropriately in the background

After a moment, Martin enters cautiously. He is dressed for travelling

Martin Knock-knock ...

Beth (*faintly; without looking at him*) Hallo. You both off, then?

Martin Sorry about this. Emergencies happen. In Ella's line, especially, you know. Specialist catering. Who'd have credited it, eh? An emergency buffet for a hundred and fifty. The day after Boxing Day. What's that about then, eh?

Beth I hope she's got some bread in.

Martin Sorry?

Beth Over Christmas. For the sandwiches. She'll need a lot of bread for a hundred and fifty.

Martin She's not going to be making sandwiches, Mum. Not for a special buffet. Sandwiches?

Beth I was going to say she can take some of ours. Our freezer's stuffed with sliced loaves ...

Martin It's fine, Mum, not to bother. As I say, I should be back this evening. In time for dinner, anyway. Traffic shouldn't be bad, Christmas Day, roads'll be fairly clear. Sorry to mess up the morning. You know ... we'd stay a bit longer and have a drink with you, only ...

Ella appears behind him in the doorway where she lingers, red-eyed

Here she is! Here she is! The girl in demand. Right. We must be off. It's a long drive ... I was telling Mum, Ella, you need to be back at work, don't you, love? ... You can't afford to lose an order like that ... not in freelance catering ... (*He pauses*) The stole looks really great. Doesn't it, Ella?

Beth Yes ...

Beth absently removes the stole from her shoulders and places it beside her on the sofa

Martin Fabulous. She's got a great eye, you know. Real flair for colours, haven't you? (*He pauses*) Tell you what, why don't we open the rest of the presents later, Mum? This evening, soon as I get back. Don't start without me, will you? No peeping. Don't you cheat, now! (*He pauses*) Well. Behave yourself while I'm gone. Fridge is full of food. One thing, you won't go hungry. She's just sorry she couldn't stay and cook it for you, you know. (*He pauses*) Well. Right. That's it then.

Beth (*after a slight pause*) See you later, love.

Martin Right. Yes. See you later. Auntie Connie still at church, is she?

Beth Yes.

Martin Say cheerio to her from Ella, then. Bye!
Beth Bye!
Martin Say goodbye to Mum, Ella.

Ella gives a tight lipped smile in Beth's direction

   Ella and Martin exit

Beth sits for a moment. She becomes aware of the TV Christmas party still in full swing

Beth Oh, shut up, just shut up, will you!

Beth points the TV remote at the set which goes off

   (*Looking at her watch*) No, she'll still be at church. Probably praying for forgiveness. I don't know what she's done to that carpet. She must have been drinking neat bleach.

Beth rises and goes to the window. She waves to the departing vehicle

   (*Mouthing*) Bye! ... Bye! Bye! ... Bye! (*Aloud*) Don't for God's sake bring her back here again, will you? Bye! Oh, no, he's still left the reindeer on, hasn't he? It'll be flashing away all day, now. (*She moves to the middle of the room and stands for a moment*) Well, I'd better get on, I suppose. So much for not lifting a finger all Christmas.

There is a clatter from the kitchen

   What was that? Hallo ... Anyone there? It's him, back again. He said he'd be back. He said he would. (*Calling; tentatively*) Gordon? Is that you? Gordon?

Another sound is heard coming from the kitchen

   I can hear you, you know, Gordon. I can't bear this, I'm going to be haunted forever. (*Listening*) It can't be him, he'd have popped up by now. Come through the floor or through the wall or something.

A faint scratching noise is heard at the kitchen hatch

   Wagstaff? (*Running to the hatch and throwing it open*) Wagsta —— !

Beth comes face to face with a very subdued Connie

(*Coolly*) Oh, it's you.

Connie (*humbly*) Sorry to disturb you.

Beth What are you doing scratching around in there?

Connie I was just getting a ——

Beth (*brusquely*) There's more red wine in the cupboard if that's what you're looking for.

Connie — a glass of water. I was just getting a glass of water, if that's all right.

Beth That's all right, help yourself.

Connie Thank you. I'm so thirsty ...

Beth Not surprised.

Connie's head disappears but the hatch remains open

(*Calling*) You go to church, then?

Connie (*off*) Yes.

Beth Enjoy it, did you?

Connie (*off*) Yes. I asked God to forgive me.

Beth Oh yes? And did he?

Connie (*off*) He's very understanding ...

Beth That's good of Him. Then it wasn't His carpet, was it?

Connie appears at the hatch

Connie Oh, Beth, I'm sorry. I'm mortified. I'm really mortified.

Beth Well, I'm sure you are, Connie. But this happens every single year, doesn't it? Year after year, love?

Connie Not every year. I'm not sick every year.

Beth No, to be fair, you're not. Last year you had a nosebleed all down the new wallpaper, didn't you?

Connie Look, I've said, I'm sorry. What more can I say?

Beth There's nothing more to be said, Connie, is there? Nothing that hasn't been said a thou —— Look, could we stop talking to each other through this hatchway, it's like visiting you in prison — either you come in here, or I'll come out there.

Connie It's all right, I'll come in there ...

Beth Please do.

Connie It's the least I can do.

Connie closes the hatch

Beth kneels on the floor by the tree and begins to sift through the presents. She pauses to glare at the tree

Beth And he never did get this thing working, did he?

Beth randomly twists one of the bulbs. The tree lights up

Oh. Right. That's fixed. Things are suddenly looking up.

Connie appears tentatively in the doorway with her glass of water

Connie (*timidly*) Knock-knock ...
Beth (*wincing*) Come in, Connie.
Connie Thank you. (*Moving to a chair*) May I sit down?
Beth Oh, for God's sake ... Sit down, Connie. Not having you tiptoeing around all Christmas, are we?
Connie I'm just so mortified, Beth. I don't know what gets into me.
Beth Connie, what gets into you are several bottles of red wine.
Connie I know ...
Beth If you're planning to start again, could you please switch to the white.
Connie I can't drink white.
Beth No?
Connie It makes me ill.
Beth Oh dear heaven. (*Still amongst the presents*) Who's this one for, it's got no label on it? Oh, yes, it's for you. Want to open it?
Connie No thank you.
Beth Here. Open it. Cheer yourself up.

Beth slides the parcel across the floor in the direction of Connie

Connie No, honestly, I can't, Beth. I couldn't open a single present, not today.
Beth Don't be so stupid, why ever not?
Connie I'm unworthy. I promised Jesus I wouldn't. As a punishment for my behaviour, I promised him I wouldn't open a single present. I'm giving them to the poor. They were given in love and as one who is not worthy of love ——
Beth (*angrily*) Oh, Connie, shut up will you? Just shut up, you stupid woman!

Silence. Connie is stunned

Sorry, I ——
Connie You've got very hard, Beth. Since his death you've grown into a hard woman, did you know that?
Beth I don't think I have. I think I'm just growing out of being soft. I'm

sorry I shouted at you, Connie. There's never an excuse for shouting, especially on Christmas Day, but ... Now, open your bloody present.

Connie obediently unwraps the gift

Connie (*staring at the contents; with a trembling voice*) It's a pair of gloves ...
Beth Oh, yes, they're nice ...
Connie (*starting to cry*) ... a pair of gloves ... somebody's gone and given me a pair of gloves ...
Beth Oh, Connie! Come on! For heaven's sake ... pull yourself together.

Beth hugs Connie for a moment

God, you're a mess, aren't you?

Connie continues to cry

Connie! Come on, now, it's just a pair of gloves.

The doorbell rings

Connie (*ceasing her crying*) What was that?
Beth Front door.
Connie Quarter past two. Who can that be?
Beth Oh, I know who it might be. I asked him to look round as soon as he'd a moment. Never expected him today, I must say.
Connie Who?
Beth (*as she goes out to the hall*) David Grinseed.

Beth exits

Connie (*alarmed*) David Grinseed? (*Dabbing at her face feverishly*) David can't see me like this ... he can't see me like this, can he ...? I need to lie down.

Connie scurries from the room after Beth

After a moment, Beth enters with David

David (*as he enters*) I came as soon as I could. As soon as I got your message ...
Beth Thank you.

David I hope this is a good time. I tried to judge things just right, between the end of lunch and the start of the Queen's speech, if you're at all into that, as I'm sure you are. Now ...

Beth I'm so sorry, I feel rather guilty. I had no intention of dragging you out, not today ...

David No, no, no. Not at all. Working day.

Beth Yes.

David Me and the Queen, both. Though I understand she tends to be pre-recorded.

Beth Oh yes, probably. Please sit down ...

David Unfortunately, it's not possible to pre-record me, I'm afraid. (*He laughs*)

Beth (*smiling politely*) No, no ...

David Much as I'd welcome it, especially come the middle of January ...

Beth Yes ...

David It gets very cold in that church ...

Beth Yes, it must do.

David With so few people ... Now, Beth. What can I do for you?

Beth (*suddenly shy again*) Well, it's bit complicated ... it's hard to put into words ... (*She hesitates*)

David (*gently*) Carry on, I'm listening.

Beth Do you ... have you — have you ever seen a ghost, David?

David No. I can't say I have, not personally.

Beth But you think they can exist?

David Possibly.

Beth I mean, you don't disbelieve in them?

David (*proceeding cautiously*) I believe some people honestly believe they've seen ghosts. I respect that. Although there's seldom concrete evidence to support or deny their claims. Not dissimilar, in a way, to flying saucers, I suppose. But then again, most of religious faith is lacking in concrete evidence — indeed that's why they're called faiths, isn't it? As a bishop I know once said, "When it comes down to it, all of it's based, in the end, on a lick and a promise, isn't it?"

Beth Only I believe I have seen one.

David A ghost?

Beth Yes. On two separate occasions.

David Recently?

Beth Oh, yes. The first time was yesterday evening at dinner, shortly after you left.

David That recently?

Beth The second time was in the night. Well, early this morning, really. About two a.m.

David Two a.m.? Weren't you asleep?

Beth No, that's the point. There was all this commotion ...

David Commotion?

Beth It doesn't matter.

David No, the point I'm making is do you think you could have been dreaming. I mean, the middle of the night?

Beth No, I could see him as clearly as I see you. He was sitting just there ——

David He?

Beth Yes.

David It was a man?

Beth It was my husband.

David Your husband?

Beth Yes. Gordon.

David Your late husband?

Beth Yes.

David The one with the — ladder?

Beth Yes.

David Did you — did you converse with him at all? Have a wifely chat?

Beth Oh yes, we talked for quite a time.

David That must have been nice for you. Reassuring.

Beth Not very, no. He kept threatening to come back, telling me that I couldn't possibly manage on my own without him, that he'd been summoned as a result of a formal request and he was here officially.

David Summoned?

Beth Yes. As the result of a formal request.

David And where did this formal request come from, did he say?

Beth Well, as far as I could understand it, from the way it was put, you know, from the wording and so on, it came from you.

David Me?

Beth Yes.

David Goodness.

Beth So what I'm saying is, I'm asking you, can you somehow reverse it?

David Reverse it?

Beth I don't want him back, you see.

David You don't?

Beth No. Not at all. I realized as soon as I saw him that it was never going to work. His dying was very sad at the time, of course it was, but it was the end of a chapter, wasn't it? Not just for him — he'd moved on to other things, hadn't he? — but for me, as well. I've got to move on. If you stay set, you know, fixed in one point, then in a way you die as well, don't you? It's just the same as dying only worse. I have to carry on as me, don't I? Do you see?

David Yes, I — think I do.

Beth I mean, don't get me wrong, I'm not suddenly going to be playing the violin or start tap-dancing but it's like, in myself, moving on. Seeing things differently. Looking at different things — differently.

David Yes. (*Tentatively*) Is Gordon here still?

Beth He's around. Somewhere.

David Can you see him at the moment?

Beth No. But he won't be far away.

David I think what you're asking me to do, Beth, is some sort of exorcism.

Beth Not really, I don't think ——

David Now, that is rather specialist stuff, you know and not really my field. In fact, in certain quarters these days, it's quite frowned upon.

Beth No, I think we can do without all the bells and the books and the candles. All I need you to do is to reverse the prayer.

David Reverse it?

Beth Say, you know, like, "Sorry, I made a mistake, she doesn't want to see him, after all. She doesn't miss him that much. It was a great marriage while it lasted but now she's just relieved to get shot of him."

David Beth, I can't believe you feel that. Look into your heart and ask yourself, do I really and truly believe that? Relieved to get shot of him?

Beth Well. Maybe that's putting it a bit strongly but — yes. He was a wonderful man in many ways, he was — yes, he was a rock, in a way. On which I felt safe to stand at first and, later, when times got hard, under which I could even shelter … But rocks, you see, well if you're not careful, they can roll on top of you, can't they, if you let them? Last few years really and truly, David, I felt — suffocated … Please.

David (*quite moved by her plea*) Yes. Perhaps we should — perhaps we should simply sit together for a minute and share a silent prayer, Beth.

Beth Right. (*Indicating the table*) Over here, be all right?

David Yes, yes. That'll be fine. Perhaps we could — sit opposite each other perhaps and ——

Beth and David sit either side of the table

Now, if we join hands, perhaps ——

Beth allows David to take both her hands

(*Closing his eyes*) That's good. Now, I want you to concentrate, Beth. Try and think of Gordon. Try to think of saying goodbye to Gordon. Waving him a fond, a loving farewell ... Thanking him for the joy he's brought into your life for the happiness you've shared together ... and above all for the selfless love, over the years, he's given to you, to your family, your fine son, his lovely girlfriend, your sister-in-law ... Let's both spare a minute, shall we, to concentrate on that ...

Beth closes her eyes

Gordon slowly rises up until he's sitting at the end of the table in his chair. He watches Beth and David

Gordon You're committing a serious error, Beth. If you go through with it, this will be the last you'll ever see of me, old girl. Just ask yourself, quite frankly and honestly, Beth, can I really manage the rest of my life without old Gordon? Can I, hand on heart, honestly say yes to that?

Beth (*in a firm, defiant whisper*) Yes!

Gordon's chair sinks down again. He goes

David (*opening his eyes*) Yes?

Beth Yes. Thank you.

They both rise a little awkwardly as a result of the experience

David (*moving to the door*) Well, I must — oh, look at the time. Must get home in time for the speech. My mother would never forgive me if I ... She's eighty-eight, you know. Still going strong. Amazing how some of them keep going, isn't it? Give my regards to your — to Connie, will you?

Beth Yes, I will. Thanks again, David.

David Don't bother, I can see myself out. Don't bother. Goodbye. Happy Christmas, Beth.

David exits

Beth Happy Christmas. (*Gazing round the room*) Well, now. What next?

From behind the hatch, a scratching sound is heard again

Oh, for heaven's sake, Connie. Would you kindly stop lurking, woman? (*Crossing to the hatch; impatiently*) He's gone now, you can come out, you stupid thing. What on earth's the point of ——

Beth starts to open the kitchen hatch. Something invisible causes the doors to fly open sharply. Beth is knocked aside as it brushes past her and, simultaneously, we hear a cat's miaow, loud and indignant

The invisible cat then does a joyous circuit of the room. We and Beth are able to follow the cat's progress due to the items that are dislodged or knocked over as the creature does this. These include the Christmas tree which topples over on its base, the fire tongs which go over with a crash into the hearth, and the occasional ornament

(*During this; incredulously*) Wagstaff? Wagstaff! You stop that, do you hear?

The circuit eventually brings Wagstaff round to his basket. There is a brief silence as the mayhem ceases. The cushion in the cat basket gently flattens into an indentation as a feline body apparently settles on to it contentedly. Beth approaches the basket tentatively with one hand extended

Wagstaff ... Wagstaff ...

Another more pleasurable miaow comes from the basket, followed by a loud purring

(*Sighing*) Oh, dear God ...

Beth sits amongst the debris, staring at the basket and shaking her head. As the invisible Wagstaff walks towards her, she scoops him up into her arms

The Lights slowly fade to Black-out

FURNITURE AND PROPERTY LIST

ACT I

On stage: Dining table
Easy chairs
Armchair
Coffee table. *On it*: tea tray containing tea things for two, biscuits
TV and remote control
Cat basket bed
Door leading to a hall
Service hatch with twin doors connecting to a kitchen
Fireplace. In it: coal-effect electric fire
Fire tongs
Sofa which converts to a bed
A few Christmas cards
Window with curtains
Sideboard. *In it*: cutlery, mats, a cruet, two new Christmas candles.
    On it: ornaments
Cupboard. In it: wine glasses
Side table. On it: table lamp
Wall socket

Off stage: Milk jug (**Connie**)
Glass of red wine (**Connie**)
Bags and boxes (**Ella**)
Artificial Christmas tree with lights attached (**Martin**)
Can of beer (**Martin**)
Re-filled glass of red wine (**Connie**)
Large toolbox (**Martin**)
Four plates of vertically presented salad (**Ella**)
Bottle of white wine, covered basket of warm bread (**Ella**)
Bottle of red wine (**Martin**)

Personal: **Martin**: car keys, lighter

ACT II

SCENE 1

Strike: Items on the table

Set: Make up sofa bed
               Restore main lights on Christmas tree
               Close curtains

Off stage: Shoes (**Martin**)

Personal: **Martin**: watch

ACT II

SCENE 2

Set: Re-assemble sofa
               Presents under Christmas tree, including gift-wrapped pair of
                  gloves
               Scraps of wrapping paper

Off stage: Glass of water (**Connie**)

Personal: **Beth**: stole, watch

LIGHTING PLOT

Practical fittings required: Christmas tree lights, table lamp

ACT I

To open:	Interior light, evening	
	Exterior street light glows through the window	

Cue 1	**Martin** clicks the wall switch	(Page 29)
	Interior lights go out	

Cue 2	Everyone gathers around **Beth** in consternation	(Page 30)
	Ghostly light upon **Gordon**	

Fade to Black-out

ACT II, Scene 1. Night-time

To open:	Table lamp	
	External lights pulse on and off	

Cue 3	**Beth**: "One … two … three …"	(Page 36)
	Table lamp switches off	

Cue 4	Kitchen hatch bursts open	(Page 36)
	Shaft of light illuminates the room	

Cue 5	**Martin**: "Happy Christmas!"	(Page 44)
	Fade to Black-out	

ACT II, Scene 2. Morning

To open:	Interior light	

Cue 6	**Beth** randomly twists one of the light bulbs	(Page 48)
	Tree lights on	

Cue 7	**Beth** scoops the invisible Wagstaff into her arms	(Page 54)
	Slow fade to Black-out	

EFFECTS PLOT

ACT I

Cue 14	**Beth**: "You all right there, love?" *Thumping continues*	(Page 25)
Cue 15	**Beth**: "… you need just to lift it slightly first, love." *Thumping continues*	(Page 25)
Cue 16	**Beth**: "Just lift it — that's it." *Thumping stops*	(Page 25)
Cue 17	**Martin** clicks the wall switch *Small bang*	(Page 29)

ACT II

Cue 18	**Beth**: "With a little bit of help from me." *Loud knock on front door;* *Doorbell rings simultaneously*	(Page 33)
Cue 19	**Martin**: "I hope to God she hasn't woken Ella …" *Knocking*	(Page 34)
Cue 20	**Man**: "She's lucky not to be locked up." *Feet walking down stairs*	(Page 34)
Cue 21	**Man**: "Thank you very much. Merry Christmas." *Front door closes*	(Page 35)
Cue 22	**Beth**: "Oh, sleep. Blessed sleep …" *Slight pause, then scratching at the kitchen hatch*	(Page 37)
Cue 23	**Beth** listens *Louder scratching at the kitchen hatch*	(Page 37)
Cue 24	**Gordon**: "Like a red rag to a bull for me, all that." *Door slams upstairs*	(Page 39)
Cue 25	**Gordon**: "Just like old times this, isn't it?" *Bump upstairs*	(Page 39)
Cue 26	**Gordon**: "Dear, oh dear!" *Bump upstairs*	(Page 41)
Cue 27	**Ella** cries *Heavy footsteps across the floor upstairs* *Door slams upstairs*	(Page 43)

Lightning Source UK Ltd.
Milton Keynes UK
UKOW06f0623170516

274404UK00015B/325/P